BEARCUB BIOS

DWAYNE JOHNSON

ACTOR AND PRO WRESTLER

by Rachel Rose

Consultant: Beth Gambro
Reading Specialist, Yorkville, Illinois

BEARPORT PUBLISHING

Minneapolis, Minnesota

Teaching Tips

BEFORE READING

- Look at the cover of the book. Discuss the picture and the title.
- Ask readers to brainstorm a list of what they already know about Dwayne Johnson, including what they learned from the cover. What can they expect to see in this book?
- Go on a picture walk, looking through the pictures to discuss vocabulary and make predictions about the text.

DURING READING

- Read for purpose. Encourage readers to look for key pieces of information they can expect to see in biographies.
- Ask readers to look for the details of the book. What happened to Dwayne Johnson at different times of his life?
- If readers encounter an unknown word, ask them to look at the sounds in the word. Then, ask them to look at the rest of the page. Are there any clues to help them understand?

AFTER READING

- Encourage readers to pick a buddy and reread the book together.
- Ask readers to name three things Dwayne Johnson has done throughout his life. Go back and find the pages that tell about these things.
- Ask readers to write or draw something they learned about Dwayne Johnson.

Credits:
Cover and title page, ©Cubankite/Shutterstock and ©BLUR LIFE 1975/Shutterstock; 3, ©Kwaku Alston/Corbis/WireImage; 5, ©Kevin Winter/Getty Images; 7, ©George Napolitano/Media Punch/Alamy; 8, ©Miami/Collegiate Images/Getty Images; 11, ©George Napolitano /Getty Images; 13, ©Michael Buckner/Getty Images; 14, ©Barry King/Getty Images; 15, ©WireImage/Getty Images; 16, ©Joe Scarnici/Getty Images; 19, ©Theo Wargo/WireImage/Getty Images; 19, ©Theo Wargo/WireImage/Getty Images; 21, ©Mike Marsland/WireImage/Getty Images; 22, ©Rich Fury/Getty Images; 23, ©George Pimentel/WireImage/Getty Images; 23, ©Krakenimages.com/Shutterstock; 23, ©Bjoern Deutschmann/Shutterstock; 23, ©YAKOBCHUK VIACHESLAV/Shutterstock

Library of Congress Cataloging-in-Publication Data

Names: Rose, Rachel, 1968- author.
Title: Dwayne Johnson : actor and pro wrestler / Rachel Rose.
Description: Bearcub bios | Minneapolis, Minnesota : Bearport Publishing
Company, 2022. | Series: Bearcub bios | Includes bibliographical
references and index.
Identifiers: LCCN 2020051860 (print) | LCCN 2020051861 (ebook) | ISBN
9781647478414 (library binding) | ISBN 9781647478490 (paperback) | ISBN
9781647478575 (ebook)
Subjects: LCSH: Johnson, Dwayne, 1972---Juvenile literature. |
Wrestlers--United States--Biography--Juvenile literature. |
Actors--United States--Biography--Juvenile literature.
Classification: LCC GV1196.J64 R67 2022 (print) | LCC GV1196.J64 (ebook)
| DDC 796.812092 [B]--dc23
LC record available at https://lccn.loc.gov/2020051860
LC ebook record available at https://lccn.loc
.gov/2020051861

For more information, write to Bearport Publishing, 5357 Penn Avenue South, Minneapolis, MN 55419. Printed in the United States of America.

Contents

Action Hero

Dwayne Johnson smiled.

He turned to the cameras.

Click, click, click!

It was time for Dwayne's new movie.

Dwayne's Life

Dwayne was born in California.

His father and his grandfather were **wrestlers**.

Growing up, Dwayne watched his father in the wrestling **ring**.

Dwayne’s father

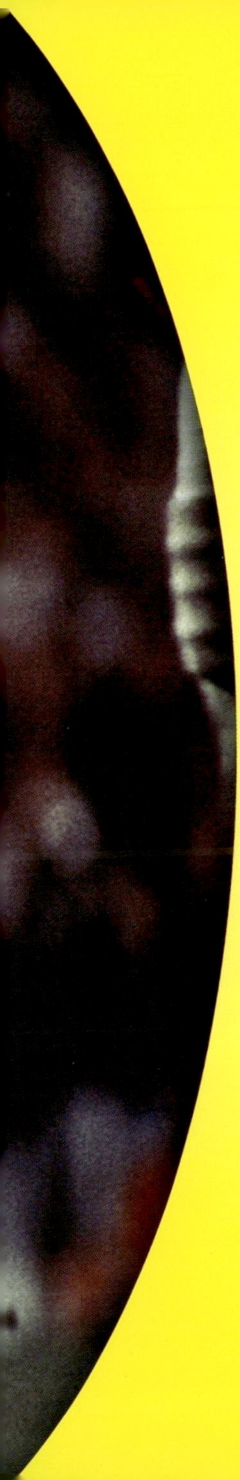

Dwayne was a big kid.

He was very strong.

He loved football.

In college, he was a great football player.

After college, Dwayne turned to wrestling.

He won a lot.

Dwayne was a big star!

His ring name was The Rock.

Then, Dwayne wanted to be an actor.

He felt **nervous**.

So he got an acting teacher.

Soon, he was a star in movies!

Dwayne was in the movie *Moana*.

He was the voice of Maui.

The part was a big deal for Dwayne.

Maui was based on Dwayne's grandfather.

ANA
REMIERE
Maui

Dwayne is a busy actor.

He has been in many movies and TV shows.

Dwayne also cares about kids.

He likes to give back.

Dwayne raises money for kids in **hospitals**.

Sometimes he meets sick kids.

He wants to make them happy.

Dwayne always does his best.

He works hard and has made himself a star.

What will he do next?

Did You Know?

Born: May 2, 1972

Family: Ata (mother), Rocky (father), Wanda (sister), Curtis (brother)

When he was a kid: His family moved around a lot. He went to high school in Hawaii.

Special fact: Dwayne eats up to seven meals a day!

Dwayne says: "Always be the hardest worker in the room."

Life Connections

Dwayne believes working hard can make your dreams come true. What are your dreams? What can you do to make them come true?

Glossary

hospitals places where people who are sick or hurt go to get better

nervous feeling worried or afraid

ring the space where people wrestle

wrestlers people in a sport where they try to get others to the ground

Index

Read More

Duling, Kaitlyn. *Dwayne Johnson (In the Spotlight).* Minneapolis: Jump!, 2019.

Stoltman, Joan. *Dwayne Johnson (Little Biographies of Big People).* New York: Gareth Stevens Publishing, 2019.

Learn More Online

1. Go to **www.factsurfer.com**
2. Enter "**Dwayne Johnson**" into the search box.
3. Click on the cover of this book to see a list of websites.

About the Author

Rachel Rose is a writer who lives in San Francisco. Her favorite books to write are those about people who lead inspiring lives.